I0817431

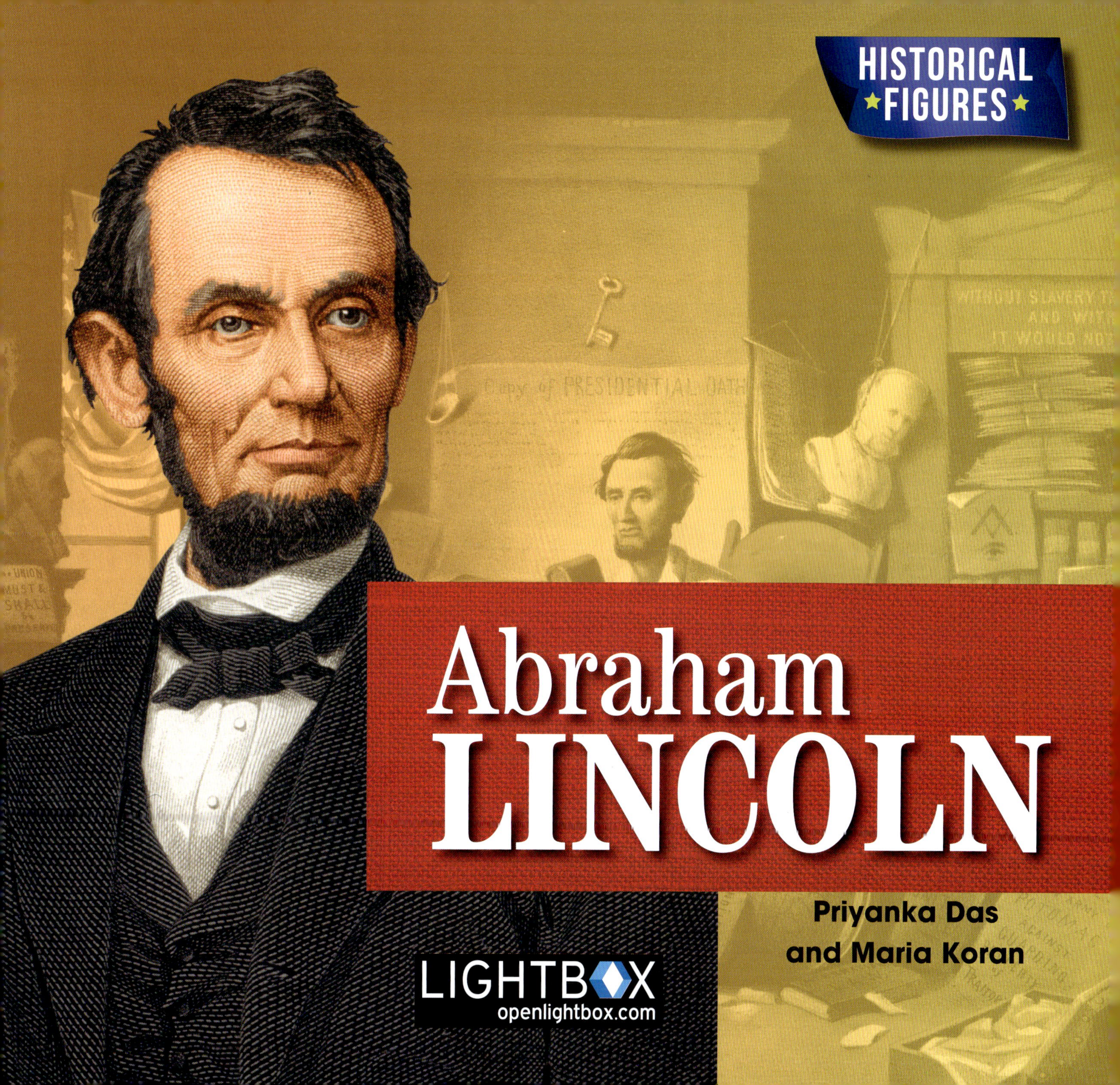
HISTORICAL
FIGURES
Abraham
LINCOLN
Priyanka Das
and Maria Koran
LIGHTBOX
openlightbox.com
Copy of PRESIDENTIAL OATH

Go to
www.openlightbox.com
and enter this book's
unique code.

ACCESS CODE

LBXF9852

Lightbox is an all-inclusive digital solution for the teaching and learning of curriculum topics in an original, groundbreaking way. Lightbox is based on National Curriculum Standards.

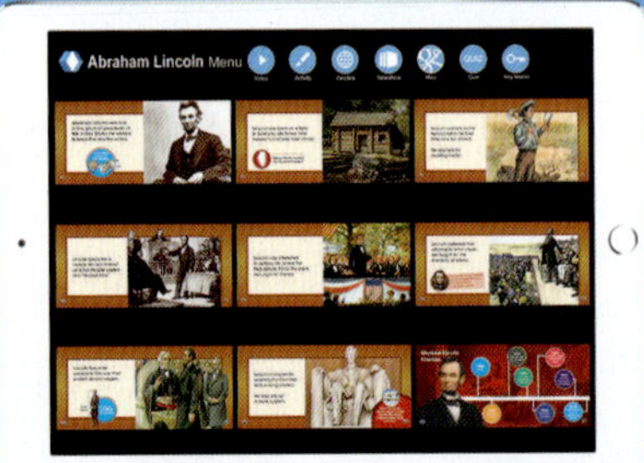

OPTIMIZED FOR

- ✓ **TABLETS**
- ✓ **WHITEBOARDS**
- ✓ **COMPUTERS**
- ✓ **AND MUCH MORE!**

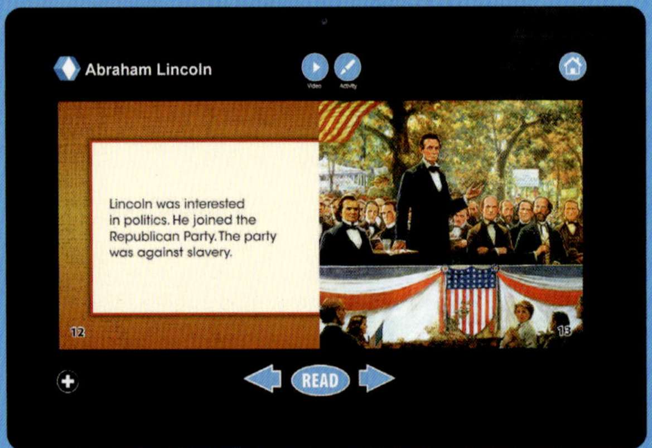

STANDARD FEATURES OF LIGHTBOX

 **AUDIO** High-quality narration using text-to-speech system

 **VIDEOS** Embedded high-definition video clips

 **ACTIVITIES** Printable PDFs that can be emailed and graded

 **WEBLINKS** Curated links to external, child-safe resources

 **SLIDESHOWS** Pictorial overviews of key concepts

 **INTERACTIVE MAPS** Interactive maps and aerial satellite imagery

 **QUIZZES** Ten multiple choice questions that are automatically graded and emailed for teacher assessment

 **KEY WORDS** Matching key concepts to their definitions

VIDEOS

WEBLINKS

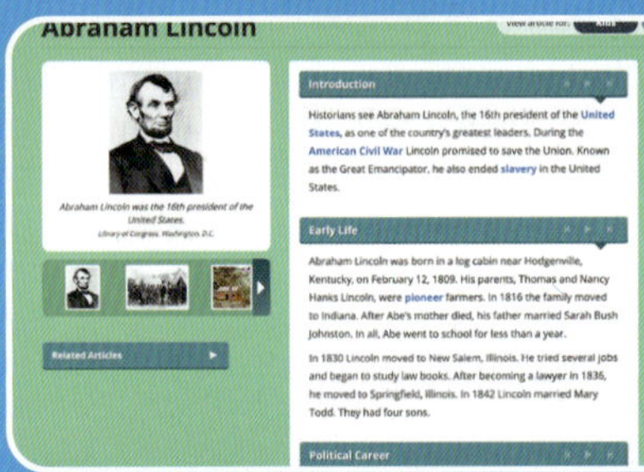

SLIDESHOWS

QUIZZES

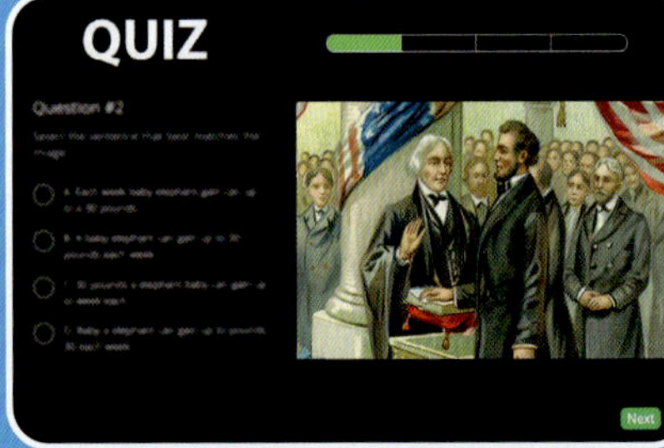

Abraham LINCOLN

Contents

Abraham Lincoln was one of the greatest presidents of the United States. He worked to keep the country united.

Lincoln was born on a farm in Kentucky. His family later moved to Indiana, then Illinois.

Today, Illinois is called the "Land of Lincoln."

Lincoln worked on his family's farm. He had little time for school.

He learned by reading books.

Lincoln became a lawyer. He was honest and fair. People called him "Honest Abe."

Lincoln was interested in politics. He joined the Republican Party. The party was against slavery.

COLES COUNTY
FOR
LINCOLN
400 MAJORITY

Lincoln believed that all people are equal. He fought for the freedom of slaves.

"Those who deny freedom to others deserve it not for themselves."
- Abraham Lincoln

Lincoln became president. The war that ended slavery began.

Lincoln was the **tallest** U.S. president.

Lincoln is known for winning the Civil War and ending slavery.

He also set up a bank system.

More than 7 million people visit the **Lincoln Memorial** in **Washington, D.C.,** each year.

Abraham Lincoln Timeline

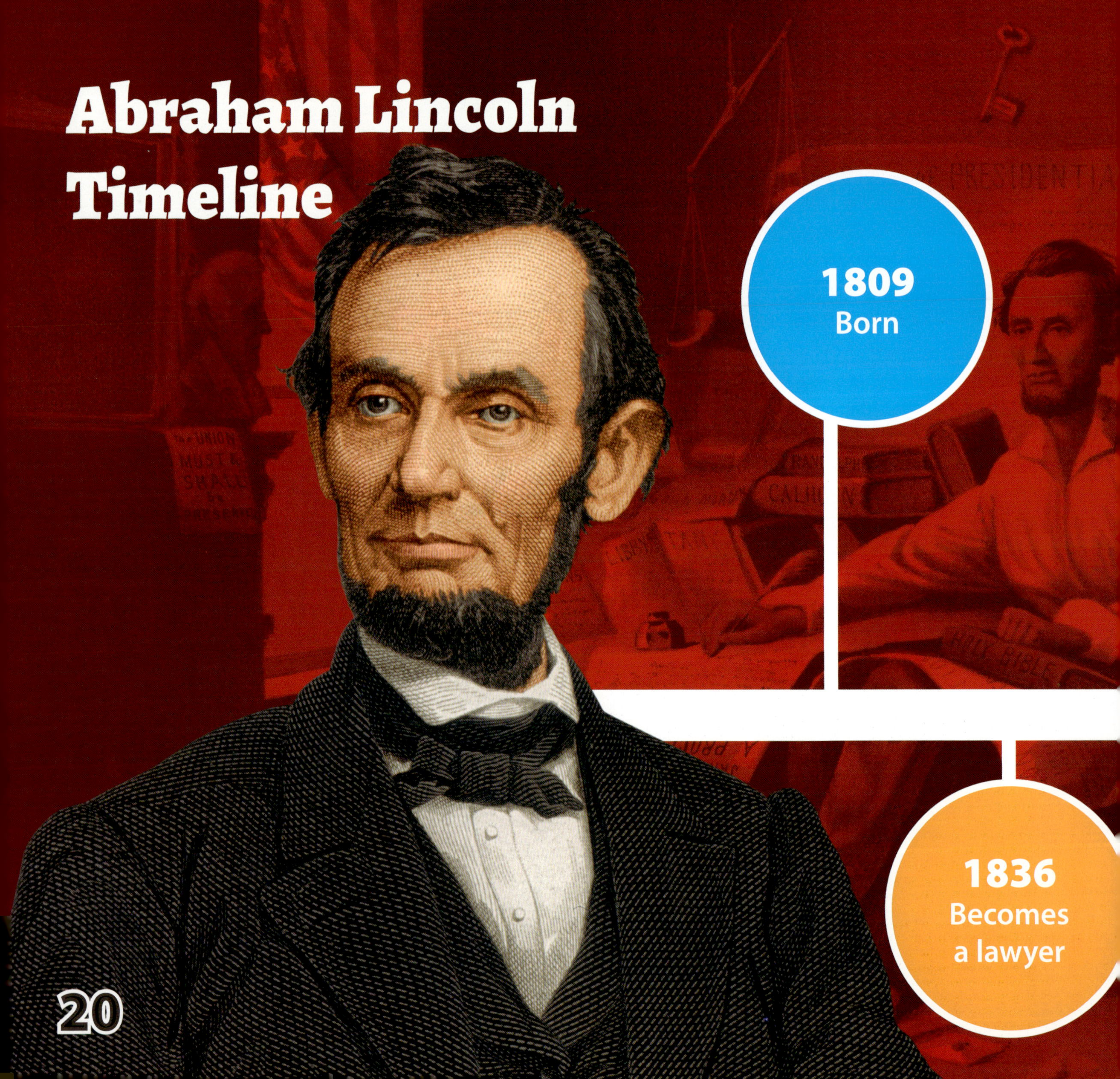

1861
Becomes 16th U.S. president

1863
Gives the Gettysburg Address

1864
Reelected president

1865
Civil War ends and Lincoln dies

1922
Lincoln Memorial is completed

2019
Giant Lincoln statue is displayed in Illinois

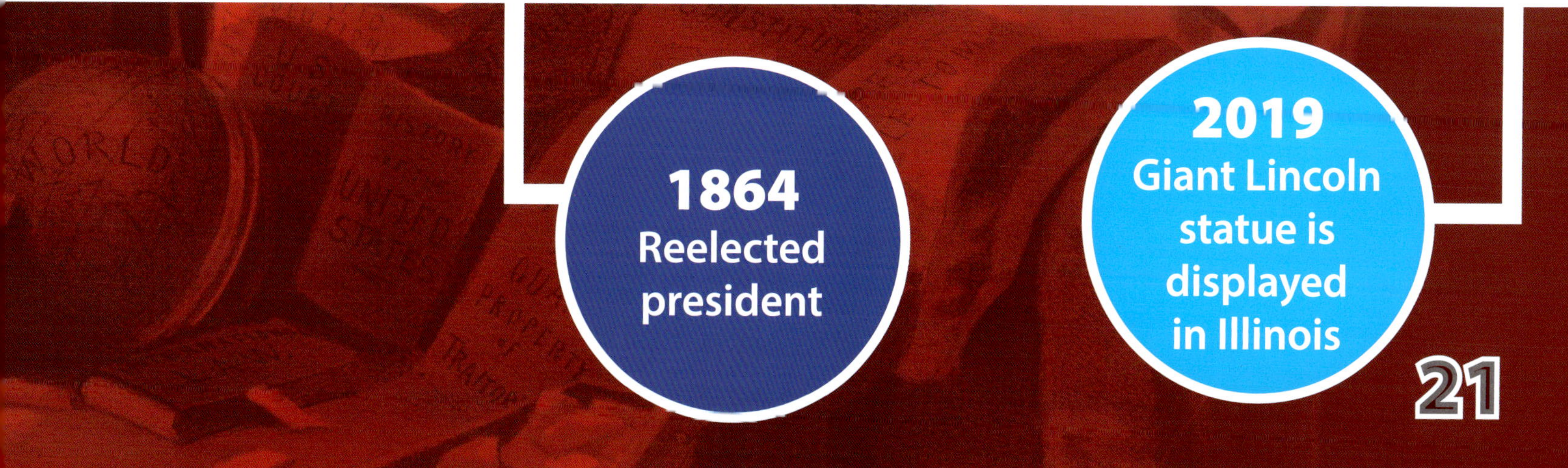

Cause
A cause is the reason something happens.
Lincoln thought that all people are equal.
Lincoln was president.

Effect

An effect is the outcome.

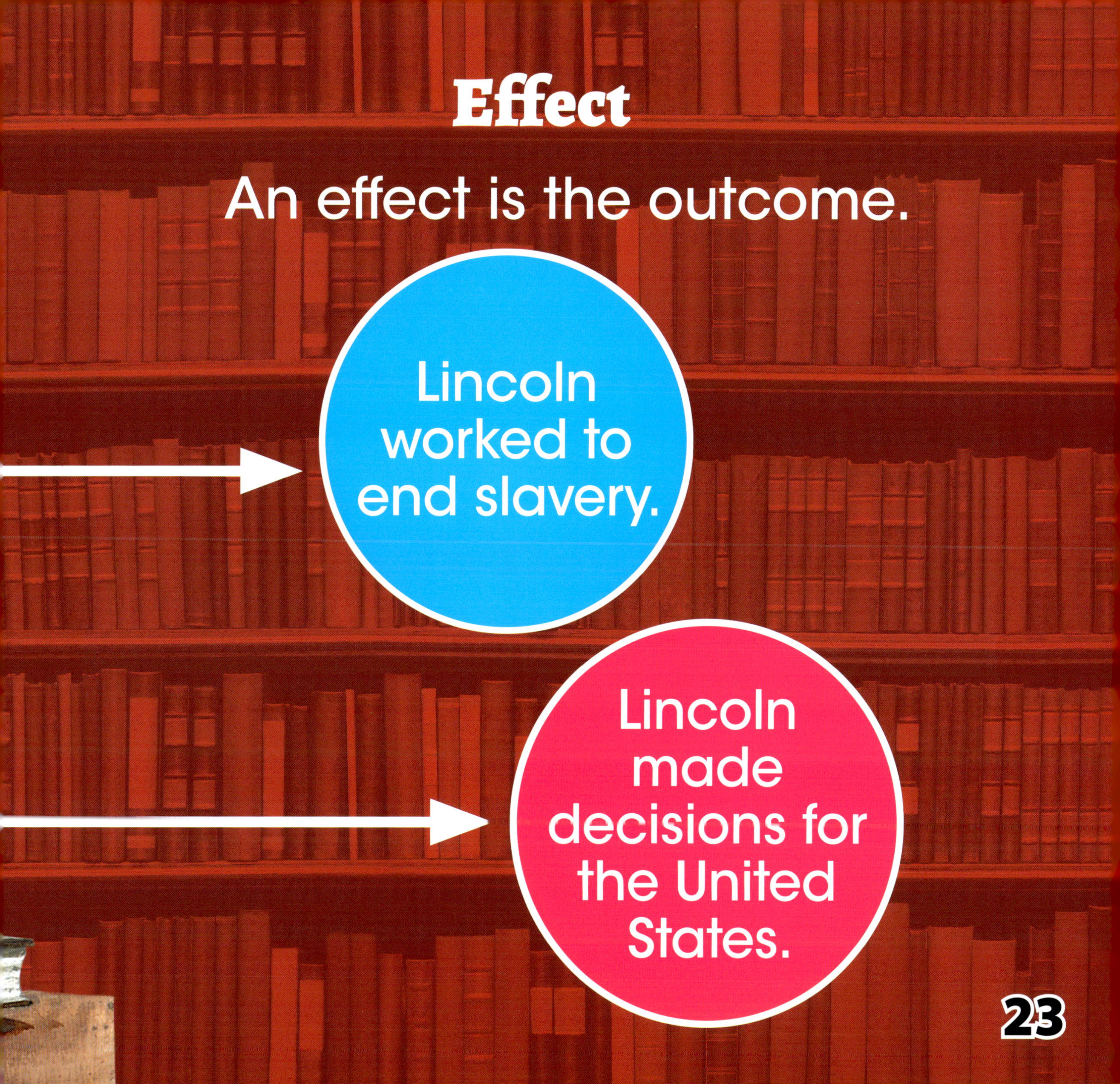

KEY WORDS

Research has shown that as much as 65 percent of all written material published in English is made up of 300 words. These 300 words cannot be taught using pictures or learned by sounding them out. They must be recognized by sight. This book contains 54 common sight words to help young readers improve their reading fluency and comprehension. This book also teaches young readers several important content words, such as proper nouns. These words are paired with pictures to aid in learning and improve understanding.

Page	Sight Words First Appearance
4	country, face, he, is, keep, of, on, one, states, the, to, was
6	a, family, farm, his, in, land, later, then
8	books, by, for, had, little, school, time
10	and, him, people
14	all, are, it, not, others, that, those, were, who
16	began, feet
18	also, set, up
19	each, more, than, year
21	ends, gives
22	something, thought
23	an, made

Page	Content Words First Appearance
4	Abraham Lincoln, money, presidents, United States
6	Illinois, Indiana, Kentucky
10	lawyer
12	politics, Republican Party, slavery
14	freedom
16	war
18	Civil War, bank system
19	Lincoln Memorial, Washington, D.C.
21	Gettysburg Address, statue
22	cause, reason
23	decisions, effect, outcome

Published by Smartbook Media Inc.
350 5th Avenue, 59th Floor New York, NY 10118
Website: www.openlightbox.com

Library of Congress Cataloging-in-Publication Data

Names: Das, Priyanka, author. | Koran, Maria, author.
Title: Abraham Lincoln / Priyanka Das and Maria Koran.
Description: New York : Lightbox, 2020. | Series: Historical figures | Audience: Ages 4-8 | Audience: Grades K-1
Identifiers: LCCN 2020014251 (print) | LCCN 2020014252 (ebook) | ISBN 9781510553750 (library binding) | ISBN 9781510553767 | ISBN 9781510553774
Subjects: LCSH: Lincoln, Abraham, 1809-1865--Juvenile literature. | Presidents--United States--Biography--Juvenile literature. | United States--History--Civil War, 1861-1865--Juvenile literature. | United States--Politics and government--1861-1865--Juvenile literature.
Classification: LCC E457.905 .D37 2020 (print) | LCC E457.905 (ebook) | DDC 973.7092 [B]--dc23
LC record available at https://lccn.loc.gov/2020014251
LC ebook record available at https://lccn.loc.gov/2020014252

Printed in Guangzhou, China
1 2 3 4 5 6 7 8 9 0 24 23 22 21 20

042020
110819

Project Coordinator: Priyanka Das
Designer: Ana María Vidal

Every reasonable effort has been made to trace ownership and to obtain permission to reprint copyright material. The publisher would be pleased to have any errors or omissions brought to its attention so that they may be corrected in subsequent printings.

The publisher acknowledges Alamy, Bridgeman, Getty Images, and iStock as the primary image suppliers for this title.